STEM - Data Storage and Communication

by Patrick H. Stakem

(c) 2017, 2022

Number 6 in the STEM Series

Table of Contents

Introduction

This book covers the topic of the storage and communications of digital data for STEM. It is addressed to the teacher, providing information and pointers to information for developing a curriculum on this topic.

Author

The author has a BSEE in Electrical Engineering from Carnegie-Mellon University, and Masters Degrees in Applied Physics and Computer Science from the Johns Hopkins University. During a career as a NASA support contractor from 1971 to 2013, he worked at all of the NASA Centers. He served as a mentor for the NASA/GSFC Summer Robotics Engineering Boot Camp at GSFC for 2 years. He taught Embedded Systems for the Johns Hopkins University, Engineering for Professionals Program, and has done several summer Cubesat Programs at the undergraduate and graduate level.

Mr. Stakem can be found on Facebook and LinkedIn. Comments, corrections, suggestions are appreciated.

Why digital data is important

Our technology is increasingly digital. Digital data is a quantitative value. It can approximate a analog (variable) or represent a digital (discrete) value. Analog data can be approximated in digital, to the accuracy required. Evidently, the word *data* in English dates back to 1640.

There were references to transmittable and store-able computer information right after World War-II. References to "data processing" emerged in 1946, as "computer" began to refer to a room full of electronics, as apposed to a person with a mechanical calculator and a slide rule. Information is organized and analyzed data; answers to questions. Information reduces uncertainty.

We live in a digital age, where everything of interest to use is digital – either sampled analog, or originating as digital. Color is continuous, a full range of analog data. What we see on a TV screen or digital camera image is sampled version of that. Our technology is based on digital; that's how we store, transmit, and process information. Thus our data is digital.

What is STEM?

STEM (Science, Technology, Engineering, Mathematics) is the key to the United States' continued dominance in High Technology. It took a lot of expertise to implement the first cell phone. Now they are turned out like cookies in third world countries.

STEM addresses overall education policy and curriculum sources in schools, at critical grade levels.

Although the teachers are experts in their particular area, and know how to present grade-appropriate material, they may not know how to find and access the advanced resources they need, or where to get help in a particular topic area.

STEM programs are seen as critically important in the

education system, world-wide. It is getting to be a complex, interconnected ecosystem. Advances in the subject areas of STEM will take place only by those who know how to exploit this ecosystem for knowledge.

When I was in school, well before the Internet and STEM age, I had an encyclopedia, updated yearly. Today, students can access Google and WikiPedia from their smart phones. The focus has changed from knowing facts, which are at your fingertips, on demand, to leveraging facts to innovate. This approach touches all of the academic disciplines, the Humanities, Languages, Art, besides the STEM topics. Perhaps the best skill set to have is good internet search skills. Teachers have had to transition from asking factual questions, to asking questions that derive from applications of online research, and accrued knowledge.

When I was a kid, there was no STEM. My interests in science and engineering led to research and hands-on experimentation. Luckily, I survived. I was called on, while in grade school, to demonstrate some concepts of electricity to a High School class. The first satellite was launched, and I was glued to the black & white TV. I participated in Model Rocketry at the High School Level, and went on to fly Nationally. This was made possible by an extraordinary High School Science teacher. I made quite a few friends, some of whom became Astronauts. I was given a great opportunity when I received a full scholarship to a College of my choice. I went to Carnegie Tech in Pittsburgh (now, Carnegie-Mellon University), and launched a career in Engineering and Aerospace. It is time for me to pay forward.

I think that Digital data storage and communications should be a major focal point for STEM, embracing a wide variety of topics at the cutting edge of technology and science. I have a handful of technical degrees, and spent 42 years at the various NASA Centers. I teach Engineering courses world-wide, and have done specialty Cubesat courses at the undergraduate and graduate level. It is time to apply that expertise earlier in the education process.

My thesis is, a project brings together all of the interesting pieces to provide a focal point for student work. There is a massive body of applicable free support material available. I have experience teaching engineering courses at the advanced undergraduate and graduate level, but I have no experience or credentials at the critical pre-K thru 12 levels.

I think STEM is a critical resource for understanding and implementing the future. I think the Digital I/O and Storage paradigm is a good thing to introduce into STEM. Let's do this. Future generations of STEM-mys will thank us.

Although STEM schools will have in-house expertise in Science (Physics, Chemistry, Biology), and Math (counting numbers through calculus), they are not heavily into Technology and Engineering. That's where you can ask for help – there's a lot of resources and knowledgeable individuals available out there.

An earlier book of mine in the STEM category addressed how computers achieve math, and how they execute instructions. A major part of this is the binary system. In this book we will briefly discuss the binary system, but focus on how the data are stored, and transmitted.

We have data that our human ancestors left for us, tens of thousands of years ago, and we can understand most of it. In the caves of Lascaux, in France, there are nicely painted images, that you realize document a successful hunt, and a great dinner. Very simple color paintings on clay. There are later examples of true writing on clay tablets in many alphabets. We can read most of these. From scratch, you need a lot of data, or you need a Rosetta stone, with the same message in three languages (and alphabets). In the basements of the Minoan Palaces in Greece, large numbers of clay tablets in various languages provide a "database" of commercial transactions. Most worrisome is the Phaistios disk, of the approximate size of a CD, with characters inscribed in a spiral (like a cd). We can't read it. There are no other examples of this writing. It is not Linear-A or -B, or Hittite, or Etruscan. It has been extensively studied, but there is only one known example of this alphabet. How long will our digital media last, and the 1's and 0's be understood?

Number representation in computing machinery

A *bit* is the smallest unit of binary information. It represents a yes/no, on/off, left/right, north/south type of decision. It can be represented in mathematics as the digits zero and one. Any technology that can represent two states can represent a bit. Red light/green light, voltage or no voltage, current or no current, light or darkness, north magnetic or south magnetic, etc. We have to be careful to distinguish between the mathematical concept of a bit (one of two possible states) and its implementation.

Because our current computation, communication, and storage technologies use 2-state devices, the binary system is the representation of choice for numbers. The binary system predates the computer age by quite a bit (no pun intended). The ancient Egyptians used binary numbers around 1650 BC. It is a positional system, like decimal. Similar use can be found in ancient India and China.

We don't necessarily need to use base-2 for computers, but it matches the implementation in current microelectronics technology fairly well. Early computers (and calculators) used base-10, which we use because we have ten fingers or toes. Binary lends itself well to translation to Octal (base-8) and hexadecimal (base-16), if you don't like long strings of 1's and 0's.

Charles Babbage's mechanical computers of the mid 19th century used decimal notation. The binary system was known, but Boole and DeMorgan hadn't worked out all the details in using logic for calculation, and there was the conversion issue. At the cost of complexity, Babbage built his machinery to do calculations in decimal. It can be seen at the Science Museum, Kensington, England. A great numeric calculator, designed to be worked by steam.

The choice of a base number in mathematics will influence how easy or hard it is to manipulate the numbers. If we just want to know that we have 1 sheep, 2 sheep, or many sheep, we don't need very sophisticated math. The ancient Babylonians used a base-60 math, which survives in the way we tell time (seconds, minutes) and measure angles. They also had computers, abacus units designed to handle their representation. The Romans did not use a positional number system, which is why it remains very hard to do long division in Roman numerals.

A *positional number system* allows us to choose a base number, and use the number digits to represent different orders of magnitude, even fractions. In Roman numerals, we have a specific symbol for fifty, and that is "L". In decimal, we use "50." That is to say, 5 x 10 (the base) plus 0 times 1. ($1 = 10^0$)

We also need to consider the important concept of zero, which was used in ancient Mesoamerica, China, India, and other places. The Romans had the concept of zero, just not a specific symbol for it. The zero symbol become important in positional notation, to keep the symbols in the right place, not just to indicate that we have no sheep.

We like to use base 10 and computers like to use base 2, so we will need to discuss how to convert numbers between these bases.

But first, why do computers use base-2. Well, Babbage's Difference engine, turned by a large hand crank, works well with decimal numbers. But is is amazingly complex, a work of art in metal. Your phone out-performs it.

The basis of modern technology is the transistor, a device that can be on or off. It is amazingly fast, doing billions (10^9) of on-off's per second. Also, we can implement billions of these on a very small piece of silicon, with photographic techniques. Our basis technology does binary math, but what we see on our screens has been translated (by software) to our familiar decimal numbers. What we type is is decimal, which get translated to binary. These two operations are done at our speed. The actual math, internal to the machine, is done at computer speeds. We don't really need to know what goes on inside, but some of us are curious er than others. Some of the students may go on to work in this field, developing more advanced technology. Here's what's going on behind the curtain. Some of this is math, some is engineering.

Bytes, words, and data structures

A *byte* is a collection of 8 bits. This makes for a handy size. In binary, a byte can represent 1 of 256 (2^8) possible states or values. 4 bits is referred to as a "nibble," half a byte. We can represent 16 numbers (2^4).

A computer *word* is a collection of 8, 16, 24, 13, 97, or some other number of bits. The number of bits collected into a word does not need to be a power of two. The range of numbers we can represent depends on how many bits we have in the word. This determines the complexity of the implementation.

In simple terms, how many 1's and 0's we have defines the biggest number we can represent.

Prefixes

There are standard metric system (SI) prefixes used to represent orders of magnitude in decimal. The same prefixes are also used to designate binary powers, but are not part of the SI system.

The prefixes are defined for decimal values, but are also applied to binary numbers. The percent difference is not much, but in the larger magnitudes, can be significant. When someone in the computer or communications industry quotes you a number of giga-somethings, stop them and ask if that is decimal or binary.

Generally, memory size is measured in the powers of two, and communication speed measured in decimal powers. Hard disk sizes are specified in decimal units. Computer clock frequencies are usually specified in decimal.

Prefix	Decimal	Binary	deviation
K = *kilo*	10^3	2^{10}	*2.4%*
M = *mega*	10^6	2^{20}	*4.9%*
G = giga	10^9	2^{30}	*7.4%*

T = tera	10^{12}	2^{40}	*10%*
P = peta	10^{15}	2^{50}	*12.6%*
E = exa	10^{18}	2^{60}	*15.3%*

To date, there has been no reported major failures related to misinterpreting or confusion over prefix units. There have been class action lawsuits regarding confusing marketing information on packaging.

Representing Letters

Besides numbers, the computer can have letters as data. In this case, we use a numeric code for the various letters. You can use any encoding for letters that you wish, but if you want a printer to understand it, you'd better use ASCII – the American Standard Code for Information Interchange. A table of the ASCII code is included later in this book.

American Standard Code for Information Interchange (ASCII) was devised for communication of symbols for teletypes from the 1960's. It is a 7-bit code with 128 possible combinations. This gives us four groups of 32: for control characters, lower case, upper case, numbers and punctuation characters. An ASCII character fits in an 8-bit byte, with one bit to spare. This is sometimes used as a parity bit, for error control.

With a parity bit, you can adjust have the entire word to have either even parity (even number of 1's) or odd parity (odd number of 1's). It the transmitter and the receiver agree on this, the receiver can detect a transmission error caused by a single bit error. Better than nothing.

Although a 7-bit code can handle the Roman alphabet, upper and lower case, it is not useful for character systems (such as Amharic) that have a large number of letter combinations, or logo=syllabic systems such as Chinese. ASCII extensions address variations in Latin letters, such as those found in Italian, Spanish, Portuguese, French, and other Latin based languages, and regional uses, such as the British Pound sign (for currency), represented on US keyboards as "#". In all cases, these "letters" are converted to bit patterns that computers can store and manipulate. Printers, with little computers embedded in them know what character to form in ink when they see these patterns.

Encoding and Decoding

When we store binary data, we group it into words. Something like the alphabet can be encoded into binary, following the ASCII code table. If we don't want some one else to read it, we can use a different translation table, one we made up. We need to give the recipient a copy of the code table, so the message can be decoded. That works well in the simple case, but the code can be broken with enough examples of the encoded text. This is based on the letter frequency, which is know for all alphabets in use. You can also use an encoding method called the one-time pad, where a random encoding is used just once. We're not gong very far into the spy stuff, just enough to supplement what we need to know about processing digital data,

Data Communications

This section discusses data communications, which allow the transfer of information from one place to another in digital format.

Moving physical messages

A message, or communication, can take the form of a physical object, sent from a source to a destination. Thousands of years ago, messages of importance traveled by courier on the roads of empires. This process evolved over time to the mail system, which relies on many technologies. In the middle ages, it was not uncommon, in the absence of a organized mail system, to locate travelers who were going in the right direction, and entrust them with the message. Carrier and homing pigeons were also used, with some success. As late as World War II, carrier pigeons were used to report on the progress of the Normandy landings. The Native American smoke signal was another communication scheme.

The mail system is a public or private system of moving letters (messages) and packages from a source to a destination. Probably closely following the invention of writing, clay tablets were carried as messages. Egyptian Pharaohs used couriers to carry messages as early as 2400 BC. Empires depended on communication.

The first postal system was developed in ancient Persia, credited to Cyrus the Great. The Persian post relied on couriers on horses and stations for changing horses along the way. The Mongolian Empire under Genghis Khan had a formal postal system. Of course, a mail system also allows for the delivery of packages as well as messages. For premium services such as U. S. Priority Mail, the envelopes and boxes are standardized. Standardization allows for more efficient handling, and is applied to shipping containers and Internet Packet traffic.

By 1842, the Baltimore & Ohio railroad was carrying government mail for $300/mile. Later, Rail Post Offices, RPO's, allowed for sorting, collecting, and distributing the mail en-route. Similar arrangements were made with steamboat companies. Mail has been transported by horse, mule, pigeon, camel, balloons, airplanes, rockets, and many other methods.

We can generalize these methods of delivery and distribution of information into the digital world, and use the post office and the telegraph and telephone system as a model for how we move information on the Internet.

At the same time, we can substitute the movement of information for the movement of physical objects. I could send you a chair, or I could tell you how to build one in a phone call or email. If you have the raw materials on hand, the instructions will facilitate the construction. With the emergence of 3-D printing, we can do even more elaborate local fabrication. The International Space Station has a 3-D printer that fashions repair parts on site that would take a while to arrive from the ground.

Pallets and packets

Standardization is the key to moving things efficiency. The cargo pallet was used in World-War two. Later, the shipping container was developed, to fit on trucks, trains, and boats. It doesn't matter if the container is filled or not, the machinery that moves it around efficiency rely's on its dimensions and lift points being the same. This is the basis for intermodal freight, which goes from ship to train to truck.

Standardization is also used by the post office. You can give them any old box under a certain weight and size limit. But it is cheaper to use their (free) priority mail boxes, for which they say, "if it fits, it ships." Amazon, who probably ships more boxes per day than any other company on the planet, has standardized box sizes. They fill in the blank volumes with bags of air.

So, in the digital world, standards also help in data movement. We use packets, not pallets, but the idea is the same. A packet is a "data envelope" that a computer word fits in. Part of the packet is the to-address, and the from-address. All the networking gear on the internet knows how to read these addresses, and get the data from point A to point B.

Routers are the piece of equipment that looks at the addresses in the packets, and forwards them along in the right direction. Routers have tables of addresses, that are updated frequently. If a certain line goes down (the pole was hit by a truck carrying containers...), a new path to the desired destination will be found. This is the magic of the original ARPAnet.

Back in Hawaii, the University system wanted to link the campus's together with data lines, so the remote campuses could use the main campus time-sharing computer. - problem was, they were on different islands. They implemented a solution in 1971, using a wireless packet-based system, based on ethernet. It operated at 9600 baud. A variation on this was developed for the Advanced Research Project Agency as a packet-switching network .

The ARPAnet was a packet switching network in 1990. Each packet, or container of information, had a header with recipient and sender information, time, size, etc. Each of these was examined by a recipient, which decided if it was relevant to them or not. If not, it was send out again. Where it was sent was determined by a routing table, a data structure in memory, giving the path to the intended recipient. This routing table changed, as nodes on the network became busy or failed. The beauty of the system was that there would be multiple paths to a recipient, so the message could get through even if cables or equipment failed. This is what the Department of Defense wanted, for their command-and control network, in case of nuclear war.

Each machine on the ARPAnet used a special computer

(refrigerator-sized) to interface their computer to the network. Each Interface Message Processor (IMP) could be programmed to connect to just about any host processor. On the other side of the IMP, a interconnecting cable linked one IMP with others. I was at Carnegie Mellon University when we got an early IMP. It was lowered through the roof of the building to the 4th floor computer center by a crane. Life was good. We could talk to other computer centers, 7 of them, I believe.

The Internet is a world-wide network of networks. Any computer can connect to the internet using hardware derived from the ARPSNET Project. These are now called routers, and have gotten much smaller. If you have internet service, you bought or leased a router from your Internet Service Provider (ISP). This links your computer to every other computer on the planet (that allows you to). Every computer has a unique host name. This maps into a series of numbers, an IP address that is unique.

TCP/IP

Transmission control protocol/Internet Protocol are networking standards used on the Internet. They date back to the DoD ARPAnet project. Their use enables end-end data communication, without concern for the intervening network. TCP/IP pre-dates the Open Systems Interconnect (OSI) model, which provides updated capability. TCP/IP is available for essentially any computer on the planet (and a few that are not.

Input/Output Implementation

This section explores the implementation of moving data around on wires, optical cables, and via radio links. There are quite a few useful protocols for hardware and software in these areas.

Digital communication interfaces in computer systems can be specialized, but most use industry-standards. The data communication can be *serial* (bit at a time) or *parallel* (many bits at a time). There is an upper limit to the distance for parallel communications due to bit skew, but serial communication can travel along a wire or optical cable, or through the atmosphere or space. Bit skew s where the strict timing of bits begins to drift.

We are going to focus on serial communications. Although most data in the computer are multi-bit words, we can ship these out a bit at a time, so they become serial.

Back in the day, when you wanted to communicate with some one at a distance, you went to the telegraph office, and printed your message on a form. The operator translated your letters to their equivalents in Morse code, and sent them as a series of switch closures. At the other end, the operator translated the clicks back to letters and punctuation. The message include a "to" and "from" section.

Morse invented the most popular telegraph code, that eventually dominated the industry. It had dots and dashes, where a dash was a longer signal, and could be distinguished by trained ear. Morse code is very resilient in a noisy environment, and gets the message through when voice can't.

Early telegraph operators, on the night shift, used to play chess games over the lines.

Now, Wireless networking such as wifi and Bluetooth, and short-range infrared (IR) are also used. Your tv remote uses an IR signal. Your phone probably talks to your car via bluetooth. More than likely, you have a wireless router in you home and work, as your local endpoint on the Internet. Special signaling codes have evolved for these different media, to optimize speed and minimize errors.

Serial Communications

Serial communications can take place at gigabit or higher rates, and does not suffer from bit skew. In addition, it can take be used over arbitrary distances, and with various carrier modulation schemes. At this moment, the Voyager spacecraft is sending data back to Earth over a serial radio frequency link, even though the spacecraft is outside the solar system, at a nominal 4 bits per second.

Serial communication of multiple bits utilizes time domain multiplexing of the communication channel, as bits are transmitted one at a time. Which bit is transmitted first? Well, there are two ways to do that, least-significant bit first (little-endian) and most significant bit first (big-endian). And, it makes no difference which you use, as long as the transmitter and receiver agree.

The serial communication parameters of interest include:

- Baud rate. (Symbol rate).
- Number of bits per character.
- Endian – MSB or LSB transmitted first.
- Parity/no parity.
- If parity, even or odd.
- Length of a stop bit (1, 1.5, 2 bits).

The baud rate gives the speed of transmission of data characters. The bit rate is the speed of individual bits making up the information and the overhead. For example, if we have 8 data bits, 3 overhead bits, and we transfer characters at 1000 baud, we are using a bit rate of 11000 bits or 1375 bytes per second.

What is the length of a bit? That is the time period of the bit, the reciprocal of the frequency. At 1000 Hertz, a bit is 1/1000 second, (1 millisecond) long.

In *synchronous communication*, a shared clock is used between the transmitter and receiver. This clock can be transmitted on a second channel, or be a shared resource, such as GPS-derived time. In synchronous systems, characters are transmitted continuously. If there is no data to transmit, a special SYN character is used to fill in.

In asynchronous communication, the transmitter and receiver have their own local clocks, and the receiver must synchronize to the transmitter clock. The receiver and transmitter clocks are usually very accurate, being derived from crystal oscillators. Clock drift between the units is less of a problem than phase drift – the receiver does not know when a transmission (and thus a bit edge) begins. This is mitigated by a protocol.

When characters are not being transmitted in an asynchronous scheme, the communications channel is kept at a known idle state, known as a "Mark", from the old time telegraph days. Morse code is binary, and the manual teletypes used the presence or absence of a voltage to represent one state, and the absence to indicate the other state. Initially, the key press or "1" state was " voltage is applied", and the resting state was no voltage. Since these early systems used acid-filled batteries, there was a desire among operators to extend the battery life, without having to continuously refill the batteries. Problem is, if the wire was cut (maliciously or accidentally), there was no indication. The scheme was changed to where the resting state was a powered state. Thus, if the line voltage dropped to zero, there was a problem on the channel, probably a cut wire, or a dead battery.

Digital circuitry currently uses 3.3 or 5 volts, and the RS-232 standard for serial communication specifies a plus/minus voltage. Usually 12 volts works fine. In any case, interface circuitry at each end of the line convert line voltage to +5/0 volts for the computer circuitry. One state is called "marking" and the other state is called "spacing". This again goes back to early (1837) Morse recording telegraphs, where one state of the line made a mark on a piece of paper tape, and the opposite state made no mark, or a space. In serial asynchronous communications, the receiver does bit re-timing. This is not required for the telegraph. Telegraphs and teletypes were essentially point-to-point or bussed systems. The lines were not switched. The voice telephone introduced the concept of circuit switching, first by manual switchboards, and later by automatic machinery. This systems required control information, in addition to the data. Sending data over analog lines was used, with the limitation of the voice-bandwidth of the lines. With clever encoding's, up to 56 kilobyte data rates were achieved. Further improvement required the abandonment of analog lines for digital lines, and brought about the Internet era. Actually, we can send analog or digital information over the same lines (copper wire, for example). The difference is in the encoding, and the transmitter and receiver units.

At idle, which is an arbitrary length period in asynchronous communication, the input assumes one known state. When it changes to another state, the receiver knows this is the start of a transmission, and the beginning or leading edge of a "start" bit. Since the receiver knows the baud rate a priori, because of a previously negotiated agreement with the transmitter, it waits one bit period to get to the first data bit leading edge, and then an additional one-half bit period to get to the middle of the bit. This is the ideal point (in communications theory terms) to sample the input bit. After, that, the receiver waits one additional bit period to sample the second bit in the center, etc., for the agreed-upon number of bits in a word. Then the receiver samples the parity bit (if the agreement allows for one), and then waits one, one and a half, or two bit periods for the "stop bits". After that, any change in the sensed bit state is the start bit of a new transmission. If the receiver and transmitter use different baud clocks, the received data will not be sensed at the right time, and will be incorrect. If the format is incorrect, for example, the receiver expects 8 data bits, and the transmitter sends 7 bits, the received word will be incorrect. This may or may not be caught by the parity bit.

Can the receiver derive clock information from the data stream, without prior knowledge of the baud rate? Yes, if special characters (sync words) are sent first. The format has to be agreed-upon. When the receiver sees a state transition(1 to 0, or vice versa) on the line, it takes this as the leading edge of the start bit. It starts a local timer, and stops the timer when the line state changes. This means the first data bit has to have the opposite state from a start bit. The receiver now knows the width of a bit, and divides this by two and starts sampling the data bits in the middle, as this is the optimum position to do so.

If special characters are used, the receiver can guess the

format of the data format to a good degree of accuracy. Given the initial guess, the receiver can transmit a request byte back to the original transmitter for a specific character, which then nails down the format. Note that this is not implemented in hardware UARTs, but can also be accomplished in software. A UART (Universal Asynchronous Receiver Transmitter) is a computer chip, or a small piece of code, that performs the function of taking an 8-bit data byte, and sending it out serially, bit-by-bit. It has to include a "start" bit parity (if used), and some stop bits to keep one serial word from bumping up against another. The receiving UART does the opposite. When it sees the start bit on the line, it clocks in the next 8 bits as data, checks the parity (if used) and sends the data word off to be stored in memory. Note that the transmitter and receiver have to be in agreement on the bit rate, parity or not, etc. Else, we get gibberish.

In *full duplex systems*, data can be sent and received simultaneously over the link. This means the communications link has to have twice the capacity of a half-duplex link, which only allows the transmission of data in one direction at a time. Each link has a practical maximum rate of transmission, which is called the communication channel capacity. It is the upper bound to the amount of information that can be successfully transferred on the channel. That depends on noise, which corrupts the received information. Claude Shannon derived the concept of channel capacity, and provided an equation to calculate it. It is related to the signal to noise ratio of the channel. Shannon is considered the Father of information theory.

In a *Master/hrlper system*, one device is master and others are helpers. The master can initiate messages to individual helper units. This scheme is typically used in buss systems. The master can also broadcast a message to all units. In a *Multi-Master* scheme there is more than one master, and an arbitration scheme is necessary. This usually is implemented with a protocol for other devices than the current master to request bus mastership, which is then granted by the master unit when feasible or convenient.

In a *Peer-Peer* scheme, on the other hand, There is no master, everyone is equal. This is the scheme used for Ethernet. If two units transmit at the same time, the transmission is garbled, and each unit retries after a random wait. When the randomness scheme works, this approach is highly effective.

Baud rate generation is handled locally at a transmitter or receiver by a crystal oscillator. It is usually 16 times the bit rate, to provide adequate sampling of the incoming signal for receivers. It can be selected to one of several values. The sample clock can be different on the receiver and transmitter, but the baud rate must be the same.

Parity is a simple error control mechanism for communications and storage. We add an extra bit to the word, so we can adjust parity. Parity is based on the mathematical concept of even (evenly divisible by two) or odd. In binary, a number is even if its least-significant (rightmost) digit is zero (0). Again, which parity you use in arbitrary, as long as the transmitter and receiver agree.

Various Interfaces

This section discusses a selection of various common communication interfaces for data.

OBD-II

This is the *on-board diagnostics* system for automobiles, based on a Bosch self-diagnostics and reporting scheme from 1969. It reports diagnostic trouble codes for the car. It's use was made mandatory by the California Air Resources Board in 1991 for emissions control systems. It is now required for cars sold in all U. S. States, and most European countries. Take a look under the steering wheel in your car, to the left. Here is the mating connector:

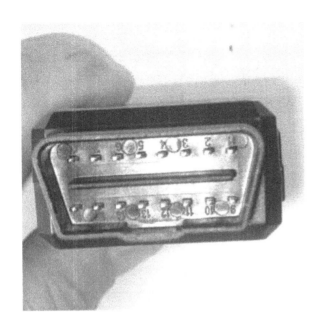

OBD-II uses the J1962 connector, the car end being located under the steering wheel in the passenger compartment. Diagnostic equipment can be linked by cable or a short-range systems such as Bluetooth. Over the interface, the CAN protocol is popular. I have an ap on my phone that talks to the OBD plug-in device in the car. If you get the dreaded check-engine light, you can get the specific code, and your phone will look it up on the internet, and tell you how to fix it.

Video

There are various schemes to handle video (high-speed data) over serial transmissions. DVI, or *Digital Visual Interface*, is a source-to-display technique, operating with a 165 MHz pixel clock. It is not analog compatible. HDMI, *High-Definition Multimedia Interface*, allows for the transmission of video and audio. It is covered by the

EIA/CEA-861 standard. It uses a 340 MHz pixel clock, and can handle standard high resolution video data. Beyond this is Sony's Gigabit video interface, GVIF, which is currently distance-limited to some 20 meters.

Serial I/O schemes, standards, and protocols

This section presents an overview of some industry standard serial communications schemes. All have an associated hardware and software specification. They may operate over different media of transmission. Their common feature is that they provide ways and means of getting bits from one point to another.

RS-232

RS-232 is a legacy electrical and functional telecomm standard dating from 1962. It has an associated EIA standard for the electrical, interface, and timing, but does not specify a connector. The 25-pin D-connector, and the 9-pin D are widely associated with RS-232.

The RS-232 scheme defines a *DTE* (data terminal device) which is a data generator/recipient and a *DCE* (data communication device) which is a channel interface device. This works well for telecomm, where we have a DTE and a DCE at each end, but if a computer is talking to a terminal, which is the DCE? This is handled by having the concept of back-to-back modems, called a *null-modem*, essentially a wire-crossover.

RS-232 runs in a minimum 3-wire scheme, but includes a

serial of control signals to facilitate interface between a device and a modem. The modem translates digital signals into analog signals compatible with the telephone system (i.e., tones in the voice band). RS-232 also has a current loop option.

The early printing teletypewriter was developed to automate the process of sending messages by teletype, which involved a skilled operator at both the transmit and receive side. The earliest teletype systems used 5-bit Baudot code, and many of the signaling or control codes in RS-232 derive from the mechanical idiosyncratic characteristics of mechanical printing teletypes, using punched paper tape as the offline storage media. In a real mechanical teletype, there is a bell character, which rings the bell to get the operator's attention.

Firewire

Firewire was invented by Apple Computer in the 1990's and implemented by Texas Instruments. It is defined by IEEE standard 1394. It is intended for high speed data, such as digital video. It has a serial bus architecture for bidirectional data transfer. It allows a master to address up to 63 peripherals. It can operate in peer-peer or multi-master mode, currently up to 3.2 gigabits per second.

USB

The *Universal Serial Bus* has a simple 4-wire configuration, 2 wires for power, and two for data. It was developed in 1995. The latest specification, USB-3, provides for up to 5 gigabits per second communication speed. USB is hub-based. There is always a master hub in the system. USB has become the interface of choice for peripherals such as the keyboard and mouse, printers, external hard drives and flash drives, scanners, cameras, and many others.

The system is designed to support 127 peripherals, but is practically limited to fewer than this. USB also supplies power, up to 0.5 amp per port. In many devices, only the power leads are used, to recharge the batteries in the device from the host. You can embed RS-232 encoding into USB, and use legacy devices for I/O on modern machines

CAN

The *Controller Area Network* (CAN) dates from 1983, and has its origins in industrial control and automation. It was developed by Robert Bosch GmbH in 1986, has been widely used in the automotive industry. It has a message-based protocol, and has a multi-master broadcast serial bus. The theoretical limit for number of devices on the bus is over 2,000, but a practical limit is about 100. It is a two-wire, half-duplex arrangement. It operates at a conservative 1 mbps, and has error detection and containment features. It is widely used in automobiles, which have multiple CAN-bus networks. The transmission talks to the engine, etc.

Ethernet

Ethernet is the circa-1973 standard for local area networking technology, widely used for inter-computer data communication. It is defined in standard IEEE 802.3. It is packet-based, and routable. That means the packets contain a destination and source address. It can be used over twisted-pair, coax cable, RF, or optical fiber. It makes use of repeaters, hubs, switches, and bridges to extend the network. The Ethernet design was developed at Xerox-PARC, based on the earlier Alohanet protocols from the University of Hawaii. Their network had several RF links between islands. .

IrDA

The *Infrared Data Association* defined this standard for short range communication by infrared carrier in free space. Don't Panic, infrared is just like microwave, but a higher frequency. Range is limited by attenuation in air. It is also a line-of-sight system. It can handle up to 1 gigabit/second, and is widely used for remote controls. You probably have 6 or 8 of those down in the couch cushions. There are standards for the data format for IR use.

Bluetooth

Bluetooth is a short-range, low-power radio networking scheme. It uses a 2400-2480 MHz carrier. It is viewed as a wireless alternative to RS-232 short-range wired serial communication. It does use advanced frequency-hopping spread-spectrum techniques. It has 79 1-MHz bands defined. It is a master-helper system, and is packet-based. Bluetooth has been widely adopted as the communication mechanism in mobile phone to headset and microphone devices. Two devices can transfer data files via Bluetooth. It is point-point. The receiver has to be "paired" with the "transmitter," to establish the link. Most newer cars use bluetooth to link with your phone for hands-free operation, and the car can use your phone's Navigation ap or access your music. Bluetooth is a single point-to-point connection, so only two devices are connected together at a given time.

Serial Encoding

American Standard Code for Information Interchange (ASCII) was devised for communication of symbols for teletypes from the 1960's. It is a 7-bit code with 128 combinations. This gives us four groups of 32: control, lower case, upper case, numbers and punctuation characters. An ASCII character fits in an 8-bit byte, with one bit to spare. This is sometimes used as a parity bit, for error control. At the time, paper tape systems supported 8 bits. Later, support was included in 9-track, reel-to-reel tape and punch cards.

Although a 7-bit code can handle the Roman alphabet, upper and lower case, numbers, punctuation, and control characters, it is not useful for character systems (such as Amharic) that have a large number of letter combinations, or logo-syllabic systems such as Chinese. ASCII extensions address variations in Latin letters, such as found in Italian, Spanish, Portuguese, French, and other languages, and regional uses, such as the British Pound sign (for currency), represented on US keyboards as "#".

Earlier codes, such as the 5-bit Baudot code (ca. 1870), used a shift mechanism to allow additional codes. The term "baud," referring to the symbol rate of transmission of information, is named for Emile Baudot, the originator of the code. Baud rate is not necessarily the same as bit rate; it depends on how many bits it takes to represent a symbol (such as a Baudot or ASCII character). Baudot code was used well into the 20th century for teleprinter equipment, particularly on the AT&T TWX network.

One of the earliest coding schemes, used in Gauss's 1833 electromagnetic telegraph, was simple binary.

An Escape sequence is initiated by a special code, the Escape character (ESC). This defines the following characters to be control characters, not encoded numbers or digits, until a second ESC is received. This is contrasted with the use of control characters that have defined functions, such as tab or carriage return (which is a typewriter term). The ESC key is still included on keyboards. Control characters usually have no displayed equivalent.

ASCII's heritage in teletype machines sometimes causes confusion in modern data communications that use the protocol. For example, teletypes needed both a carriage return (CR) and a line feed (LF) at the end of a line. Non-mechanical systems can do both operations with just a CR. The "Bell" character, designed to ring the Teletypes

Bell at the receiving end for attention (or annoyance) is not frequently used anymore.

Data Storage

This section discusses the topic of storage of digital information. Memory

There are many types of memory used with the current cpu's. Most memory types are supported, if the word sizes and timing match. There is a small amount of memory on the CPU chip itself. This would be the various registers, and cache memory. Most of the primary memory is placed on the same circuit board as the cpu, and can be soldered in place, or can take the form of plug-in modules. This memory is random-access. Non-volatile memory retains its contents without applied power. Some of it will be persistent, read-only memory, but more will be read-write, volatile memory. Secondary memory, with rotating magnetic disks, may be used along with optical disks for large offline storage. Flash memory, a type of persistent storage, is considered as an alternative to disks and CD/DVD's, for back-up.

Computer memory is organized in a hierarchy. We would like to have large amounts of low power, fast, non-volatile storage. These requirements are mutually exclusive. The memory closest to the CPU is fast, random-access, volatile, and semiconductor-based, but expensive. Secondary storage, such as disk, is slower, cheaper, persistent, and cheaper on a cost-per-bit basis.

Backup storage, offline optical or magnetic, is still cheaper per bit, but may have a longer access time.

Other characteristics of interest include memory latency, the time it takes to access the requested item, and throughput, the read or write rate of the memory device. Some memory may have a relatively slow latency, but a very high throughput, once things get going.

All-in-all, we have come a long way since computers stored bits as acoustic waves in a pool of mercury, circa World War-II.

RAM

In RAM, random access memory, any element is accessible in the same clock time, as opposed to sequential media, such a tape or a disk. In sequential media, the access time varies, and depends on the order of access. This is true for disks, where the item requested probably just went by the read heads, and another rotation of the platter is required. Mechanical systems, in operation, tend to wear out due to mechanical causes. Electrical systems wear out as well, usually in a longer time.

A memory can be considered as a black-box with two functions, read and write. With the write function, we present the memory with two inputs: the data item, and an address. There is no output. The memory associates the data item with the address and remembers it. On the read function, we present the memory with the address, and expect to get back the data item previously associated with it.

Other design choices in memory include volatility. The memory may forget after a period of time. That's not good. Although, depending on the timing, the data can be read out and written back just in time, a process called refreshing.

Is there such a thing as totally non-volatile memory? One of the earliest memory types, magnetic core, was persistent when the power was turned off. It is unclear how long the data was retained. When compact disks, an optical media, first came out, the advertised lifetime was reported as 100 years. This has since been reduced, with some cd's and dvd's becoming unreadable in a period of several years. (A dvd is a cd with a greater capacity, because the wavelength of the laser light used is smaller, so the bits are closer together). If you want to see persistent color graphical information, the cave paintings at Lascaux in France are more than 17,000 years old, and still maintain their meaning. Magnetic hard disks do not forget their contents when the power is turned off. If they are properly stored, and not exposed to bumps, magnetic fields, and extremes of temperature, they seem to have the best data retention characteristics of currently available media. Exchangeable floppy disks have alignment problems in their readers, and magnetic tape drives use a fragile media that is susceptible to damage and environmental effects. These technologys are considered extinct and end-of-life. Hopefully, all useful information has been moved to newer devices.

Back in the early days of NASA, there was no world wide data network. Data received at remote stations was recorded on analog tape, and mailed back to NASA's data center at Goddard Space Flight Center in Greenbelt, Md. They were then stored in a warehouse. Unfortunately, not a climate-controlled warehouse. Most of the early records are unreadable.

Volatile memory includes static semiconductor ram and dynamic ram. Static ram uses a flip-flop, and retains its contents as long as the power remains. Static ram is faster, less dense, and consumes more power than dynamic ram. Dynamic RAM is more dense, usually by a power of 4, due to a simpler structure, but requires refresh. It forgets in fractions of a second, because the information is stored as a charge on a capacitor, which leaks away. Why would anyone use this as a storage media? It is cheap, easily mass produced, the "forget" time is eons to a computer chip, and the overhead of the refresh operation is minimal. The CPU usually does the refresh, because the memory is not usable during that time. The memory can be organized into sections, so a refresh in one section still allows access in others. Some DRAM is self-refreshing.

Non-volatile memory includes various types of read-only memory, and battery-backed static ram which has a life of several years, depending on the battery source.

Even read-only memory is written at least at once. Actually, a ROM (read-only memory) can be manufactured with a specific pattern of 1's and 0's built in. For prototyping, various types of programmable read-only memory are used. These can be written and erased multiple times. Earlier, ultraviolet light was used to erase the devices to an all-1's state. These chips had glass windows. Later, the contents became re-programmable or alterable with higher voltage levels, and could be modified in-circuit. Both the ultraviolet-erasable versions (UV-PROM's) and the Electrically alterable forms (EEPRoms) tended to forget over a period of years. Before this phenomenon was understood, these types of parts were included in shipped systems, that failed in later use. The IBM AT's BIOS was one example, and similar embedded systems were used for certain subway fare card machines.

The evolution of this is flash memory. Flash can be programmed in-circuit, and is random-access for read. To write flash, a block is erased to all "1", and selected bits are written to "0". The write operation is slower than the read. In addition, although the device can be read indefinitely, there is an upper limit to the number of times it can be written. This is on the order of millions of times in current technology, but this can be accomplished in under a second with an error. Flash memory does wear out.

Write-only memory is of no particular interest.

Memory organization and addressing

Semiconductor memory, like all current microelectronics, is a 2-dimensional structure. Thus, density usually goes up by a factor of four, as we double the width and the height. Memory is a very regular structure, amenable to mass production.

In random access memory we address bytes, or words. We get a collection of bits every time we read memory. To address individual bits within a word, we need to use the logical operations (AND, OR) to single out bits within a word.

Caches

A cache is a temporary memory buffer for data. It is placed between the processor and the main memory. The cache is smaller, but faster than the main memory. Being faster, it is more expensive, so it serves as a transition to the main store. They may be several levels of cache (L1, L2, L3), the one closest to the processor having the highest speed, commensurate to the processor. That closest to the main memory has a lower speed, but is still faster than the main memory. The cache has faster access times, and becomes valuable when items are accessed multiple times. Cache is transparent to the user; it has no specific address.

We may have different caches for instructions and data, or a unified cache for both. Code is usually accessed in linear fashion, but data items are not. In a running program, the code cache is never written, simplifying its design. The nature of accessing for instructions and data is different. On a read access, if the desired item is present in a cache, we get a cache hit, and the item is read. If the item is not in cache, we get a cache miss, and the item must be fetched from memory. There is a small additional time penalty in this process over going directly to memory (in the case of a miss). Cache works because, on the average, we will have the desired item in cache most of the time, by design.

Cache reduces the average access time for data, but will increase the worst-case time. The size and organization of the cache defines the performance for a given program. The proper size and organization is the subject of much analysis and simulation.

Caches introduce indeterminacy in execution time. With cache, memory access time is no longer deterministic. We can't tell, a priori, if an item is or is not in cache. This can be a problem in some real-time systems.

A working set is a set of memory locations used by a program in a certain time interval. This can refer to code or data. Ideally, the working set is in cache. The cache stores not only the data item, but a tag, which identifies where the item is from in main memory. Advanced systems can mark ranges of items in memory as non-cacheable, meaning they are only used once, and don't need to take up valuable cache space.

For best performance, we want to keep frequently-accessed locations in fast cache. Also, cache retrieves more than one word at a time, it retrieves a "line" of data, which can vary in size. Sequential accesses are faster after an initial access (both in cache and regular memory) because of the overhead of set-up times.

Writing data back to cache does not necessarily get it to main memory right away. With a write-through cache, we do immediately copy the written item to main memory. With a write-back cache, we write to main memory only when a location is removed from the cache.

Caches, then, provide a level of performance increase at the cost of complexity This process is transparent to the running computer program.

Cache hierarchy

This includes the L1, L2, L3 caches. L1 is the smallest and fastest cache, located closest to the cpu, usually on the same chip. Some cpu's have all three levels on chip. Each of the levels of cache is a different size and organization, and has different policies, to optimize performance at that point.

A key parameter of cache is the replacement policy. The replacement policy strategy is for choosing which cache entry to overwrite to make room for a new data. There are two popular strategies: random, and least-recently used (LRU). In random, we simply choose a location, write the data back to main memory, and refill the cache from the new desired location. In least recently used scenario, the hardware keeps track of cache accesses, and chooses the least recently used item to swap out.

As long as the hardware keeps track of access, it can keep track of writes to the cache line. If the line has not been written into, it is the same as the items in memory, and a write-back operation is not required. The flag that keeps track of whether the cache line has been written into is called the "dirty" bit. This book does discuss the dirty bits of computer architecture.

Cache organization

In a fully-associative cache, any memory location can be stored anywhere in the cache. This form is almost never implemented. In a direct-mapped cache, each memory location maps onto exactly one cache entry. In an N-way set-associative cache, each memory location can go into one of n sets. Direct mapped cache has the best hit times. Fully associative cache has the lowest miss rates.

The Cloud

Large amounts of storage, accessible from anywhere, is a widely accepted paradigm, enabled by the Internet. Data Warehouses, accessible from anywhere, with requisite security are becoming the norm for individuals and companies alike. The customer pays a fixed monthly fee for access to the data, and the hosting company assumes the responsibility for storage, backup, and accessibility.

Miscellaneous topics

This section will discuss interesting, obsolete topics, in the area of , "how we got to the digital age." Any of these could serve as a research topic for students.

Telephone

The voice telephone system is attributed to Alexander Graham Bell. The first working set-up was point to point. Many of these systems were put in place, but it evolved into a system where central switching could connect a phone to any other phone. These were manually operated switchboards, where a physical connection was made by the operator after finding out the destination from the call originator. Voice communication (analog) was more effected by noise than Morse (digital), but it could be used by unskilled operators.

Telegraph

The telegraph system evolved from point-to point systems that facilitated railway operations, and commerce. The telegraph required a skilled operator to transmit the signal in Morse code, and another skilled operator to translate the received message back to natural language. In this sense, the skilled operators were the channel modems. The on/off signaling of Morse could get a message through a noisy environment.

As an example, the Western Telegraph Co. was incorporated in Maryland in 1847. It ran a line from

Baltimore to Western Maryland in 1848. The B&O Railroad granted use of their right-of-way along the tracks for the telegraph line, which, opened in July of 1848. The railroad quickly adopted the telegraph to coordinate train movements over their single-tracked lines.

Telex

The telex network, circa 1930, used a switched network of teleprinters to send text messages. This replaced an earlier generation of point to point teleprinters for business use. The telex and printing terminals evolved from the telegraph system. The Telex system did not share wires with the telephone system, and terminals had their own unique identifying number, similar to a phone number. Telex was used internationally. The encoding scheme was the International Telegraph Alphabet Number two, and the lines operated at 50 baud. Later, the aging telex equipment was interfaced with the telephone network via modem. The network was used to send telegrams, or cablegrams. Telex was superseded by email as a message handling system.

Carrier Pigeons

Carrier, or homing pigeons, have been used to carry small messages for millennia. They were used to carry the names of the Olympic winners in ancient Greece, and were employed in a regular mail service between Baghdad and Syria in the 1100's. There is documented evidence of Persian King Cyrus using carrier pigeons in the 6th century BC. They were still used regularly into the 21st century.

Pigeons can carry up to about 75 grams, enough for a written message, or, now, a multi-gigabyte flashdrive. Pigeons can provide a backup messaging systems when all else fails, in the case of a large natural disaster.

CTAM

Chevy Truck Access Method was a favored scheme in the mainframe era of computers to move large volumes of tapes and disk packs from storage to data centers. As with IP, the latency is large, but the data transmission rate is high. (I did not make this up...)

It is left to the reader to compare and contrast the latency and bandwidth of a transcontinental optical fiber versus a 747 freighter filled with DVD's traveling from LaGuardia to LAX airports.

Near-Earth Network

The Near Earth Network (NEN) communicates with near-Earth orbiting satellites (out to Lunar orbit). It uses the NASA ground stations. There are two stations in Florida, in proximity to the Kennedy Center launch site, at the launch facility at Wallops Island, Virginia, and at the McMurdo Base in Antarctica. In addition, other commercial ground stations can be used, under contract to NASA. Goddard Space Flight Center in Greenbelt, Maryland, manages the NEN, which was formally know as the Ground Network (GN). The dish antennae of the GN range from 34 meters to 70 meters in diameter.

Space Network

The Space Network (SN) dates back to the early 1980's, when NASA introduced a constellation of satellites to replace the ground tracking stations.

The Tracking and Data Relay Satellites, in geosynchronous orbit, are the Space Segment (SS) of the SN. They implement communications between to low Earth orbiting spacecraft, and one of the TDRSS ground segments. The ground segment units are located at White Sands, New Mexico, and on Guam Island, in the Pacific. White Sands also serves as the controlling station for the TDRS spacecraft. The TDRS network was declared operational in 1989. STDN stations at Wallops Island, Bermuda, Merritt Island (FL), Ponce de Leon (FL), and Dakar, Senegal, remained operational.

The Tracking & Data Relay Satellite System is over 30 years old, and is being refreshed with new technology. The Space Segment has spare satellites in orbit in case of failure.

Deep Space Network

NASA's Deep Space Network consists of three sites spaced around the planet. It supports deep space missions for NASA and other entities. It is managed by the Jet Propulsion Lab (JPL) in Pasadena, California.. The nearest station to JPL is at Goldstone, in the desert to the east. Two other stations, in Spain and Australia are spaced about 120 degrees apart on the globe from Goldstone. The DSN started operations in the 1960's, with teletype communications with the Pasadena facility. The DSN is heavily used, but can provide backup to the Space Network for contingencies.

The Interplanetary Internet

Data communication is not limited to one planet or even this solar system. The Voyager spacecraft, launched in 1977, are still sending back data from deep space. The *New Horizons* mission to Pluto and the Kuiper Belt began in January of 2006, and reached the vicinity of Pluto in July 2015. It conducted a 6-month survey of Pluto, and went out farther into the Kuiper belt, on an 3 year extended mission, which is ongoing at this writing. In 2015, the Pluto flyby occurred, and data began to flow back to Earth. It took a year for all the imaging data to be transmitted, due to distances and available transmit power.

CCSDS

The Consultive Committee on Space Data Standards specifies standards for equipment and data formats for space missions. CCSDS Packets are used on near-Earth and Deep Space communication links. These have more rigorous error detection and correction schemes. The data length is variable, and can be from 7 to 65,542 bytes, which includes the header. Packet sizes are fixed length. The transmission of packets is via data frames, which are also fixed length. The frame also contains control information. The data frames are legacy components of NASA's space communication segment.

Trans-Atlantic cable

The first transatlantic telegraph cable was laid in 1854, and completed by 1858. Before this was operational, the quickest a message could travel between Europe and the United States was by physical message, carried by ship. The cable linked the major business centers of New York and London, via Newfoundland. It has been called the victorian Internet.

The Atlantic Telegraph Company headed the effort. The cable weighted over a ton per nautical mile, and was manufactured in England.

The communication over the cable was by Morse code, with an initial speed of 2 minutes per character. London became the communications center of the world, with cables stretching to the far ends of the British Empire. Today's undersea cables use fibre optic technology, and employ repeaters to boost the signal in the cable.

TWX

TWX, or teletypewriter exchange service, was an AT&T service in the United States, operating at 45 baud. It used the Baudot code, and a later version used ASCII. TWX operated into the 1970's. Twx was transmitted over the telephone network, with special area codes. Western Union acquired the TWX network. TWX used the Bell systems 101 dataset modem to interface to the analog phone system. A connection between the TWX network and Telex was available in 1966, which extended the reach worldwide.

Fax

Facsimile provided a way of scanning and transmitting images of documents over the telephone system. It is still used today in the Internet age, because, legally, a faxed signature is recognized by law, but an electronic signature generally isn't. Standard desktop computer equipment can handle generating, transmitting, and receiving faxes. Fax can also work over radio networks. The speed of transmission depends on the media and the modulation scheme, but ranges from 2400 baud to 64k baud. The receiving machine can print the incoming fax. This was originally done on limited-life thermal paper, but is now commonly done on plain paper, on one the computer.

Software Defined Radio

In software defined radio, once the signal is received and converted to a lower frequency, it can be processed by DSP software algorithms, implemented in software. This takes the place of a hardware approach, which does not have the flexibility provided by software. Besides the implementation, there is nothing really new about SDR. It does provide easier updates and more flexibility. A popular open source product is call GNU Radio.

Wrap-up

Some of us choose to communicate via the written word, with a lot of references that are available on the Internet. Along the same lines, the text of this book is stored on my desktop, as well as Amazon's Servers, somewhere in the Cloud.

Bibliography

Bates, Regis J., Gregory, Donald W. *Voice & Data Communications Handbook*, Fifth Edition, 2017, ISBN-0072263350.

Carla, Mooney *Big Data: Information in the Digital World with Science Projects for Kids,* August 2018, Nomad Press, ASIN-B078L6H14F.

Forouzan, Behrouz A. *Data Communications and Networking*, 5th Edition, 2012, ISBN-0073376221.

González-Bailón, Sandra *Decoding the Social World: Data Science and the Unintended Consequences of Communication*, 2017, MIT Press, ASIN-B078HVQ6Q8.

Gralla, Preston, *How the Internet Works*, 2016, ISBN-0789736268.

Hafner, Katie *Where Wizards Stay Up Late: The Origins Of The Internet,* 1998, ISBN-0684832674.

Held, Gilbert *Understanding Data Communications* (7th Edition) , 2002, ISBN-0672322161.

Horak, Ray *Telecommunications and Data Communications Handbook*, 2008, ISBN-0470396075

Levine, John R.; Levine Young, Margaret *The Internet For Dummies*, 2015, ISBN-1118967690.

Lipschultz, Jeremy Harris *Social Media Communication: Concepts, Practices, Data, Law and Ethics*, 2014, ISBN-1138776459.

McNamara, John E. *Technical Aspects of Data communication*, 1977, Digital Press, ISBN-0-932376-01-0.

Olejniczak, Stephen P. *Telecom For Dummies*, 2006, ISBN-047177085X.

Sklar, Bernard *Digital Communications, Fundamentals and Applications*, 2nd ed, 2001, Prentice Hall, ISBN 0-13-084788-7.

Shannon, Claude *A Mathematical Theory of Communication*, 1948, Bell Systems Technical Journal, July, October, 1948.

Standage, Tom *The Victorian Internet: The Remarkable Story of the Telegraph and the Nineteenth Century's On-line Pioneers*, 2014, ISBN-162040592X .

Starosielski, Nicole *The Undersea Network,* 2015, Duke University Press, ASIN-B00WO58MBI.

Stallings, William *Data and Computer Communications* (9th Edition), Prentice Hall; August 13, 2010, ISBN 0131392050.

Watson, Clyde *Binary Numbers (Young Math Books)*, 1977, Harper Collins, ISBN-0690009933.

Zlatanov, Nikola *Computer Engineering, Data Storage, Networking and Security*, 2017, ASIN-B0745YFQ8L.

Resources

- http://stem.hcoe.net/2017/11/binary-number-basics/
- Space Math - https://spacemath.gsfc.nasa.gov/
- A Brief History of the Internet, http://www.isoc.org/internet/history/brief.shtml.
- Wikipedia, various.

Glossary of terms

1's complement – a binary number representation scheme for negative values.

2's complement – another binary number representation scheme for negative values.

2-wire – twisted pair wire channel for full duplex communications. Still needs a common ground.

#G, 4G – standards for mobile telecommunications.

802.11 – a radio frequency wireless data communications standard.

Algorithm – a specification or process for solving problems.

Analog – concerned with continuous values.

ANSI – American National Standards Institute

ArpaNet – Advanced Research Projects Agency (U.S.), first packet switched network, circa 1968.

ASCII - American Standard Code for Information Interchange, a 7-bit code; developed for teleprinters.

Async – asynchronous; using different clocks.

Baud rate – symbol rate; may or may not be the same as bit rate.

Baudot – a five-bit code used with teleprinters. Obsolete.

BCD – binary coded decimal. 4-bit entity used to represent 10 different decimal digits; with 6 spare states.

Big-endian – data format with the most significant bit or byte at the lowest address, or transmitted first.

Binary – using base 2 arithmetic for number representation.

BIST – built-in self test.

Bit – smallest unit of digital information; two states.

Bit skew – where the rigid timing of the bits begins to drift.

Bluetooth – short range open wireless communications standard.

Boolean – a data type with two values; an operation on these data types; named after George Boole, mid-19th century inventor of Boolean algebra.

Buffer – a temporary holding location for data.

Bus – data channel, communication pathway for data transfer.

Byte – ordered collection of 8 bits; values from 0-255

CAN – controller area network.

Carrier – a high frequency radio signal that can be modulated with a signal.

Chip – integrated circuit component.

Cipher – algorithm to encrypt or decrypt a code word.

Clock – periodic timing signal to control and synchronize operations.

CMOS – complementary metal oxide semiconductor; a technology using both positive and negative semiconductors to achieve low power operation.

Code – transforming information into another representation.

Complement – in binary logic, the opposite state.

Cots – commercial, off-the-shelf.

CPU – central processing unit.

CRC – cyclic redundancy code, an error-control mechanism.

Cryptology – dealing with codes and ciphers.

Data – collected facts or values

Database – organized collection of data.

Datagram – message on a packet switched network; the delivery, arrival time, and order of arrival are not guaranteed.

Deadlock – a situation in which two or more competing actions are each waiting for the other to finish, and thus neither ever does.

Data Warehouse – a very large repository of data.

DCE – data communications equipment; interface to the network.

Demodulator – removes the signal from the carrier.

Digital – using discrete values for representation of states or numbers.

DSP – digital signal processing.

DTE – data terminal equipment; communicates with the DCE to get to the network.

DVI – digital visual interface (for video).

EIA – Electronics Industry Association.

Embedded system – a computer systems with limited human interfaces and performing specific tasks. Usually part of a larger system.

Ethernet – 1980's networking technology. IEEE 802.3.

Exabytes – 10^{18} or 2^{60}

File – a container of information, usually stored as a one dimensional array of bytes.

Firewire –serial communications protocol (IEEE-1394).

Firmware – computer code contained in a non-volatile memory.

Floppy drive – a disk drive using soft, insertable media. Originally 8", the 5 1/4", the 3 1/2" diameter,

Full duplex – communication in both directions simultaneously.

Giga - 10^9 or 2^{30}

GPIO – general purpose input output

GPS – global positioning system (U.S.) system of navigation satellites.

GSN – Global System for Mobile Communications by European Telecommunications Standards Institute.

Half-duplex – communications in two directions, but not simultaneously.

Handshake – co-ordination mechanism.

Hot plug – to connect equipment without turning the power off first.

I^2C – inter-integrated circuit; a multi-master serial single-ended computer bus invented by Philips.

IEEE – Institute of Electrical and Electronic Engineers. Professional organization and standards body.

IETF – Internet Engineering Task Force

IMP – Interface Message Processor – node element on the ArpaNet.

Information – analyzed data

Interrupt – an asynchronous event to signal a need for attention (example: the phone rings).

I/O – Input-output from the computer to external devices, or a user interface.

IP – intellectual property; also internet protocol.

IR – infrared, 1-400 terahertz. Perceived as heat.

ISO – International Standards Organization.

ISP – Internet Service Provider.

Kilo – a prefix for 10^3 or 2^{10}

LAN – local area network.

Latency – time delay.

LED – light emitting diode.

List – a data structure.

Little-endian – data format with the least significant bit

or byte at the highest address, or transmitted last.

LSB – least significant bit or byte.

Mac – media access control; a mac address is unique on a network.

Master-helper – control process with one element in charge. Master status may be exchanged among elements.

Mega - 10^6 or 2^{20}

Mesh – a highly connected network.

Microcontroller – microprocessor with included memory and/or I/O.

Microprocessor – a monolithic cpu on a chip.

MIL-STD-1553 – military standard (US) for a serial communications bus for avionics.

Modem – modulator/demodulator; digital communications interface for analog channels.

Modulation – the process of varying a periodic waveform with information to be sent. See, carrier.

MSB – most significant bit or byte.

Multiplex – combining signals on a communication channel by sampling.

NFC – near field communications. Range-limited.

Nibble – 4 bits, ½ byte.

NIST – National Institute of Standards and Technology (US), previously, National Bureau of Standards.

Noise – a signal you have no interest in.

NSFnet - National Science Foundation Network.

Null modem – acting as two modems, wired back to back. Artifact of the RS-232 standard.

Nyquist rate –the minimum sampling rate, equal to twice the highest frequency in the signal.

Octal – base 8 number.

Open source – methodology for hardware or software development with free distribution and access.

Packet – a small container; a block of data on a network.

Parallel – sending multiple bits at a time down multiple channels (or wires).

Paradigm – a pattern or model

Paradigm shift – a change from one paradigm to another. Disruptive or evolutionary.

Parallel – multiple operations or communication proceeding simultaneously.

Parity – an error detecting mechanism involving an extra check bit in the word.

PATA – a pc-era parallel interface, used with floppys, hard drives, and cd's

PCM – pulse code modulation.

Peta - 10^{15} or 2^{50}

Pinout – mapping of signals to I/O pins of a device.

PWM – pulse width modulation.

Queue – first in, first out data buffer structure; hardware of software.

Reset – signal and process that returns the hardware to a known, defined state.

Router – networking component for packets.

RS-232 – EIA telecommunications standard (1962), serial with handshake.

SATA – serial ATA, a storage media interconnect.

SCADA – Supervisory Control and Data Acquisition – for industrial control systems.

Semiconductor – material with electrical characteristics between conductors and insulators; basis of current technology processor and memory devices.

Semaphore –software signaling element among processes.

Serial – bit by bit.

Server – a computer running services on a network.

Shannon number – 10^{120} – Shannon's estimate of the game-tree complexity of chess.

Software – set of instructions and data to tell a computer what to do.

Snoop – monitor packets in a network

Spread spectrum – a modulation scheme where the bandwidth of the signal is spread in the frequency domain, for noise control and security.

State machine – model of sequential processes.

Symbol - A character representing an idea, concept, or object. May had a header, trailer, error detection.

Symbol rate – the rate at which symbols are transmitted and received.

Synchronous – using the same clock to coordinate operations.

System – a collection of interacting elements and relationships with a specific behavior.

System of Systems – a complex collection of systems with pooled resources.

Table – data structure in memory. Can be multi-dimensional.

Tera - 10^{12} or 2^{40}

TCP/IP – transmission control protocol/internet protocol; layered set of protocols for networks.

Transceiver – receiver and transmitter in one box.

Triplicate – using three copies (of hardware, software, messaging, power supplies, etc.). for redundancy and error control.

Truncate – discard. Cutoff, make shorter.

TTL – transistor-transistor logic in digital integrated circuits. (1963)

UART – universal asynchronous receiver-transmitter. Parallel-to-serial; serial-to parallel device with handshaking.

UDP – User datagram protocol; part of the Internet

Protocol.

USART – universal synchronous (or) asynchronous receiver/transmitter.

USAF – United States Air Force.

USB – universal serial bus.

Vector – single dimensional array of values.

Wiki – the Hawaiian word for "quick." Refers to a collaborative content website.

Word – a collection of bits of any size; does not have to be a power of two.

If you enjoyed this book, you might also be interested in some of these.

Stakem, Patrick H. *16-bit Microprocessors, History and Architecture*, 2013 PRRB Publishing, ISBN-1520210922.

Stakem, Patrick H. *4- and 8-bit Microprocessors, Architecture and History*, 2013, PRRB Publishing, ISBN-152021572X,

Stakem, Patrick H. *Apollo's Computers,* 2014, PRRB Publishing, ISBN-1520215800.

Stakem, Patrick H. *The Architecture and Applications of the ARM Microprocessors,* 2013, PRRB Publishing, ISBN-1520215843.

Stakem, Patrick H. *Earth Rovers: for Exploration and Environmental Monitoring,* 2014, PRRB Publishing, ISBN-152021586X.

Stakem, Patrick H. *Embedded Computer Systems, Volume 1, Introduction and Architecture*, 2013, PRRB Publishing, ISBN-1520215959.

Stakem, Patrick H. *The History of Spacecraft Computers from the V-2 to the Space Station*, 2013, PRRB Publishing, ISBN-1520216181.

Stakem, Patrick H. *Floating Point Computation*, 2013, PRRB Publishing, ISBN-152021619X.

Stakem, Patrick H. *Architecture of Massively Parallel Microprocessor Systems*, 2011, PRRB Publishing, ISBN-1520250061.

Stakem, Patrick H. *Multicore Computer Architecture*, 2014, PRRB Publishing, ISBN-1520241372.

Stakem, Patrick H. *Personal Robots*, 2014, PRRB Publishing, ISBN-1520216254.

Stakem, Patrick H. *RISC Microprocessors, History and Overview,* 2013, PRRB Publishing, ISBN-1520216289.

Stakem, Patrick H. *Robots and Telerobots in Space Applications*, 2011, PRRB Publishing, ISBN-1520210361.

Stakem, Patrick H. *The Saturn Rocket and the Pegasus Missions, 1965,* 2013, PRRB Publishing, ISBN-1520209916.

Stakem, Patrick H. *Visiting the NASA Centers, and Locations of Historic Rockets & Spacecraft,* 2017, PRRB Publishing, ISBN-1549651205.

Stakem, Patrick H. *Microprocessors in Space*, 2011, PRRB Publishing, ISBN-1520216343.

Stakem, Patrick H. Computer *Virtualization and the Cloud*, 2013, PRRB Publishing, ISBN-152021636X.

Stakem, Patrick H. *What's the Worst That Could Happen? Bad Assumptions, Ignorance, Failures and Screw-ups in Engineering Projects, 2014,* PRRB Publishing, ISBN-1520207166.

Stakem, Patrick H. *Computer Architecture & Programming of the Intel x86 Family, 2013,* PRRB Publishing, ISBN-1520263724.

Stakem, Patrick H. *The Hardware and Software Architecture of the Transputer,* 2011,PRRB Publishing, ISBN-152020681X.

Stakem, Patrick H. *Mainframes, Computing on Big Iron,* 2015, PRRB Publishing, ISBN- 1520216459.

Stakem, Patrick H. *Spacecraft Control Centers,* 2015, PRRB Publishing, ISBN-1520200617.

Stakem, Patrick H. *Embedded in Space, 2015,* PRRB Publishing, ISBN-1520215916.

Stakem, Patrick H. *A Practitioner's Guide to RISC Microprocessor Architecture,* Wiley-Interscience, 1996, ISBN-0471130184.

Stakem, Patrick H. *Cubesat Engineering,* PRRB Publishing, 2017, ISBN-1520754019.

Stakem, Patrick H. *Cubesat Operations*, PRRB Publishing, 2017, ISBN-15076717X.

Stakem, Patrick H. *Interplanetary Cubesats*, PRRB Publishing, 2017, ISBN-1520766173 .

Stakem, Patrick H. Cubesat Constellations, Clusters, and Swarms, Stakem, PRRB Publishing, 2017, ISBN-1520767544.

Stakem, Patrick H. *Graphics Processing Units, an overview*, 2017, PRRB Publishing, ISBN-1520879695.

Stakem, Patrick H. *Intel Embedded and the Arduino-101, 2017,* PRRB Publishing, ISBN-1520879296.

Stakem, Patrick H. *Orbital Debris, the problem and the mitigation*, 2018, PRRB Publishing, ISBN-*1980466483.*

Stakem, Patrick H. *Manufacturing in Space*, 2018, PRRB Publishing, ISBN-1977076041.

Stakem, Patrick H. *NASA's Ships and Planes*, 2018, PRRB Publishing, ISBN-1977076823.

Stakem, Patrick H. *Space Tourism*, 2018, PRRB Publishing, ISBN-1977073506.

Stakem, Patrick H. *STEM – Data Storage and Communications*, 2018, PRRB Publishing, ISBN-

1977073115.

Stakem, Patrick H.   *In-Space Robotic Repair and Servicing*, 2018, PRRB Publishing, ISBN-1980478236.

Stakem, Patrick H. *Introducing Weather in the pre-K to 12 Curricula, A Resource Guide for Educators*, 2017, PRRB Publishing, ISBN-1980638241.

Stakem, Patrick H. *Introducing Astronomy in the pre-K to 12 Curricula, A Resource Guide for Educators*, 2017, PRRB Publishing, ISBN-198104065X.

Also available in a Brazilian Portuguese edition, ISBN-1983106127.

Stakem, Patrick H. *Deep Space Gateways, the Moon and Beyond*, 2017, PRRB Publishing, ISBN-1973465701.

Stakem, Patrick H. *Exploration of the Gas Giants, Space Missions to Jupiter, Saturn, Uranus, and Neptune*, PRRB Publishing, 2018, ISBN-9781717814500.

Stakem, Patrick H. *Crewed Spacecraft*, 2017, PRRB Publishing, ISBN-1549992406.

Stakem, Patrick H. *Rocketplanes to Space*, 2017, PRRB Publishing, ISBN-1549992589.

Stakem, Patrick H. *Crewed Space Stations,* 2017, PRRB Publishing, ISBN-1549992228.

Stakem, Patrick H. *Enviro-bots for STEM: Using Robotics in the pre-K to 12 Curricula, A Resource Guide for Educators,* 2017, PRRB Publishing, ISBN-1549656619.

Stakem, Patrick H. *STEM-Sat, Using Cubesats in the pre-K to 12 Curricula, A Resource Guide for Educators*, 2017, ISBN-1549656376.

Stakem, Patrick H. *Lunar Orbital Platform-Gateway*, 2018, PRRB Publishing, ISBN-1980498628.

Stakem, Patrick H. *Embedded GPU's*, 2018, PRRB Publishing, ISBN- 1980476497.

Stakem, Patrick H. *Mobile Cloud Robotics*, 2018, PRRB Publishing, ISBN- 1980488088.

Stakem, Patrick H. *Extreme Environment Embedded Systems,* 2017, PRRB Publishing, ISBN-1520215967.

Stakem, Patrick H. *What's the Worst, Volume-2*, 2018, ISBN-1981005579.

Stakem, Patrick H., *Spaceports*, 2018, ISBN-1981022287.

Stakem, Patrick H., *Space Launch Vehicles*, 2018, ISBN-1983071773.

Stakem, Patrick H. *Mars*, 2018, ISBN-1983116902.

Stakem, Patrick H. *X-86, 40ᵗʰ Anniversary ed*, 2018, ISBN-1983189405.

Stakem, Patrick H. *Lunar Orbital Platform-Gateway*, 2018, PRRB Publishing, ISBN-1980498628.

Stakem, Patrick H. *Space Weather*, 2018, ISBN-1723904023.

Stakem, Patrick H. *STEM-Engineering Process*, 2017, ISBN-1983196517.

Stakem, Patrick H. *Space Telescopes*, 2018, PRRB Publishing, ISBN-1728728568.

Stakem, Patrick H. *Exoplanets*, 2018, PRRB Publishing, ISBN-9781731385055.

Stakem, Patrick H. *Planetary Defense*, 2018, PRRB Publishing, ISBN-9781731001207.

Patrick H. Stakem *Exploration of the Asteroid Belt*, 2018, PRRB Publishing, ISBN-1731049846.

Patrick H. Stakem *Terraforming*, 2018, PRRB Publishing, ISBN-1790308100.

Patrick H. Stakem, *Martian Railroad*, 2019, PRRB Publishing, ISBN-1794488243.

Patrick H. Stakem, *Exoplanets,* 2019, PRRB Publishing, ISBN-1731385056.

Patrick H. Stakem, *Exploiting the Moon,* 2019, PRRB Publishing, ISBN-1091057850.

Patrick H. Stakem, *RISC-V, an Open Source Solution for Space Flight Computers,* 2019, PRRB Publishing, ISBN-1796434388.

Patrick H. Stakem, *Arm in Space*, 2019, PRRB Publishing, ISBN-9781099789137.

Patrick H. Stakem, *Extraterrestrial Life*, 2019, PRRB Publishing, ISBN-978-1072072188.

Patrick H. Stakem, *Space Command*, 2019, PRRB Publishing, ISBN-978-1693005398.

CubeRovers, A Synergy of Technologys, 2020, PRRB Publishing, ISBN-979-8651773138.

Robotic Exploration of the Icy moons of the Gas Giants. 2020, PRRB Publishing, ISBN- 979-8621431006

Hacking Cubesats, 2020, PRRB Publishing, ISBN-979-8623458964.

History & Future of Cubesats, PRRB Publishing, ISBN-979-8649179386.

Hacking Cubesats, Cybersecurity in Space, 2020, PRRB Publishing, ISBN-979-8623458964.

Powerships, Powerbarges, Floating Wind Farms: electricity when and where you need it, 2021, PRRB Publishing, ISBN-979-8716199477.

Hospital Ships, Trains, and Aircraft, 2020, PRRB Publishing, ISBN-979-8642944349.

2020/2021 Releases

CubeRovers, a Synergy of Technologys, 2020, ISBN-979-8651773138

Exploration of Lunar & Martian Lava Tubes by Cube-X, ISBN-979-8621435325.

Robotic Exploration of the Icy moons of the Gas Giants, ISBN- 979-8621431006.

History & Future of Cubesats, ISBN-978-1986536356.

Robotic Exploration of the Icy Moons of the Ice Giants, by Swarms of Cubesats, ISBN-979-8621431006.

Swarm Robotics, ISBN-979-8534505948.

Introduction to Electric Power Systems, ISBN-979-8519208727.

Centros de Control: Operaciones en Satélites del Estándar CubeSat (Spanish Edition), 2021, ISBN-979-8510113068.

Exploration of Venus, 2022, ISBN-979-8484416110.

Patrick H. Stakem, *The Search for Extraterrestial Life,* 2019, PRRB Publishing, ISBN-1072072181.

The Artemis Missions, Return to the Moon, and on to Mars, 2021, ISBN-979-8490532361.

James Webb Space Telescope. A New Era in Astronomy, 2021, ISBN-979-8773857969.

Riverine Ironclads, Submarines, and Aircraft Carriers of the American Civil War, 2019, ISBN- 978-1089379287.

www.ingramcontent.com/pod-product-compliance
Lightning Source LLC
Chambersburg PA
CBHW031247050326
40690CB00007B/990